CONTENTS

INTRO

Since the 1850s the beachside suburb of St Kilda has been a popular residential and recreational spot for Melburnians. Initially favoured by the wealthy, the suburb has been home to a socio-economically diverse range of residents over the years, resulting in an equally diverse range of residential and commercial architecture appearing throughout the suburb's history.

From Edwardian and Victorian mansions, Art Deco and Spanish Mission apartments, through to Mid-Century Modern flats, St Kilda has arguably the most eclectic collection of architectural styles of any location in Australia.

The Footpath Guide to St Kilda showcases a diverse range of significant architectural buildings along a comfortably easy walk through this attractive bayside suburb.

INHABITED BY INDIGENOUS PEOPLE OF THE KULIN NATION FOR OVER 35,000 YEARS, THE AREA NOW KNOWN AS ST KILDA WAS FIRST SETTLED BY EUROPEANS IN 1839.

HISTORY

The name itself came from a schooner, the 'Lady of St Kilda', which sailed from England to Port Phillip in 1841 and spent most of that year moored at the main beach.

St Kilda soon became a popular home for wealthy settlers and, with the development of a railway line connecting the suburb to Melbourne city in 1857, was made even more popular as a recreational destination, especially during the summer months.

By the 1880s St Kilda had become Melbourne's favourite seaside playground with its pier promenade, numerous privately run sea baths (both hot and cold) and over 15 hotels including the George (1857) and the Esplanade (1878). An economic depression in the 1890s resulted in fortunes being lost and many of the St Kilda mansions were subdivided into boarding house or apartment accommodation. By the turn of the century most wealthy people had moved to more exclusive suburbs such as Brighton and Toorak and, with the opening of a new cable tram line from central Melbourne, the area became a more popular seaside retreat for the working class.

IN 1906 ITALIAN NATIVE CARLO CATANI, CHIEF ENGINEER OF THE PUBLIC WORKS DEPARTMENT, WAS TASKED WITH PREPARING A REDEVELOPMENT PLAN FOR THE ST KILDA FORESHORE.

The resulting leisure based precinct eventually featured landmarks such as the St Kilda Sea Baths (1910), Luna Park (1912), and The Palais Theatre (1927).

St Kilda's fortunes once again turned during the 1930s, with the effects of the Great Depression creating an environment ripe for the exploitative activities of crime, prostitution and drug abuse.

This was also the era when many of the high density residential apartments and flats began rising throughout the suburb, representing the popular Art Deco and Spanish Mission styles of the time.

By the late 1950s the area had become a magnet for bohemianism and alternative lifestyles as artists and various social fringe dwellers made St Kilda a vibrant and exciting, if sometimes sleazy, centre of creativity.

Luna Park

The reputation of St Kilda as a colourful, arty, grungy seaside suburb continued throughout the 1960s, 70s and 80s until the inevitable gentrification of the 1990s when inner city yuppie types replaced the hippies as the dominant demographic.

1 2 Acland St / 1940

PRINCE OF WALES HOTEL

The original Prince of Wales Hotel opened as a guesthouse on the present corner site in 1862. In 1936 it was rebuilt to a design by architect RH McIntyre. The new building, done in the contemporary Art Moderne style, opened in 1940 and soon became popular with American soldiers stationed in Melbourne during the Second World War.

Although the overall design is restrained it includes ornate decorative detailing, particularly in the etched-glass windows which depict a triple feather motif, the symbol of the Prince of Wales.

Throughout the 1970s and 80s the hotel became a major live music venue, particularly for the alternative scene, and for a few years was home to independent radio station 3PBS-FM.

After a major refurbishment in the 1990s the Prince Complex was opened that includes a boutique hotel and health spa.

✪ OF NOTE

The George / 125 Fitzroy St

Originally established as the Terminus Hotel in 1857, the George Hotel has evolved from a complex of buildings erected on the same site over a period of years from the 1870s to the 1920s. The four story corner building that stands today was constructed in 1886 as an addition to the existing hotel facing Fitzroy Street (altered in the 1920s). Designed by architect Harry B. Gibbs, it is an example of the Italianate 'Boom Style' architecture that was so popular at the time, with its Corinthian order pilasters and Renaissance loggias on the second and third storeys.

Purchased by Frederick Wimpole in 1873, the hotel remained in the same family until it was sold in 1958. In 1976 it was renamed The Seaview and became a centre for Melbourne's punk and alternative music scene, playing host to such influential acts as The Birthday Party (featuring Nick Cave), INXS, Hunters and Collectors and The Go-Betweens.

Closing in 1987, it re-opened in the 1990s after major restoration and remodelling as an apartment complex with bars, restaurants and a function room.

2 17-27 Fitzroy St / 1920

SUMMERLAND MANSIONS

The land on which Summerland Mansions stands was one of the first Crown Land parcels to be sold in St Kilda in 1842. A mansion, named Summerland House, was built on the site shortly afterwards and, in 1919, was purchased by ER and GHC Crespin.

Architect Christopher Cowper was appointed to redevelop the site and designed a block of flats incorporating retail space at street level. Completed in 1921, the resulting style is an interesting blend of Inter-war Stripped Classical, Mediterranean and Arts and Crafts.

Comprising twelve flats, six shops and a communal dining room at ground level, the complex was aimed at a wealthy clientele with its spacious interiors, luxurious detailing and generous views.

✪ OF NOTE

Tolarno's / 42 Fitzroy St

The Tolarno Hotel started out as a 19th century mansion but, like so many in the St Kilda area, has been adapted over the years for a multitude of purposes. Converted to a boarding house in the 1890s, by the 1930s it had become a private hotel and was purchased by Georges Mora and his wife Mirka in 1965.

Migrating from France in 1951, the Moras were both great patrons and practitioners of the visual arts and were well known in Melbourne's artistic circles, regularly socialising with key figures such as Albert Tucker, Sidney Nolan and Arthur Boyd.

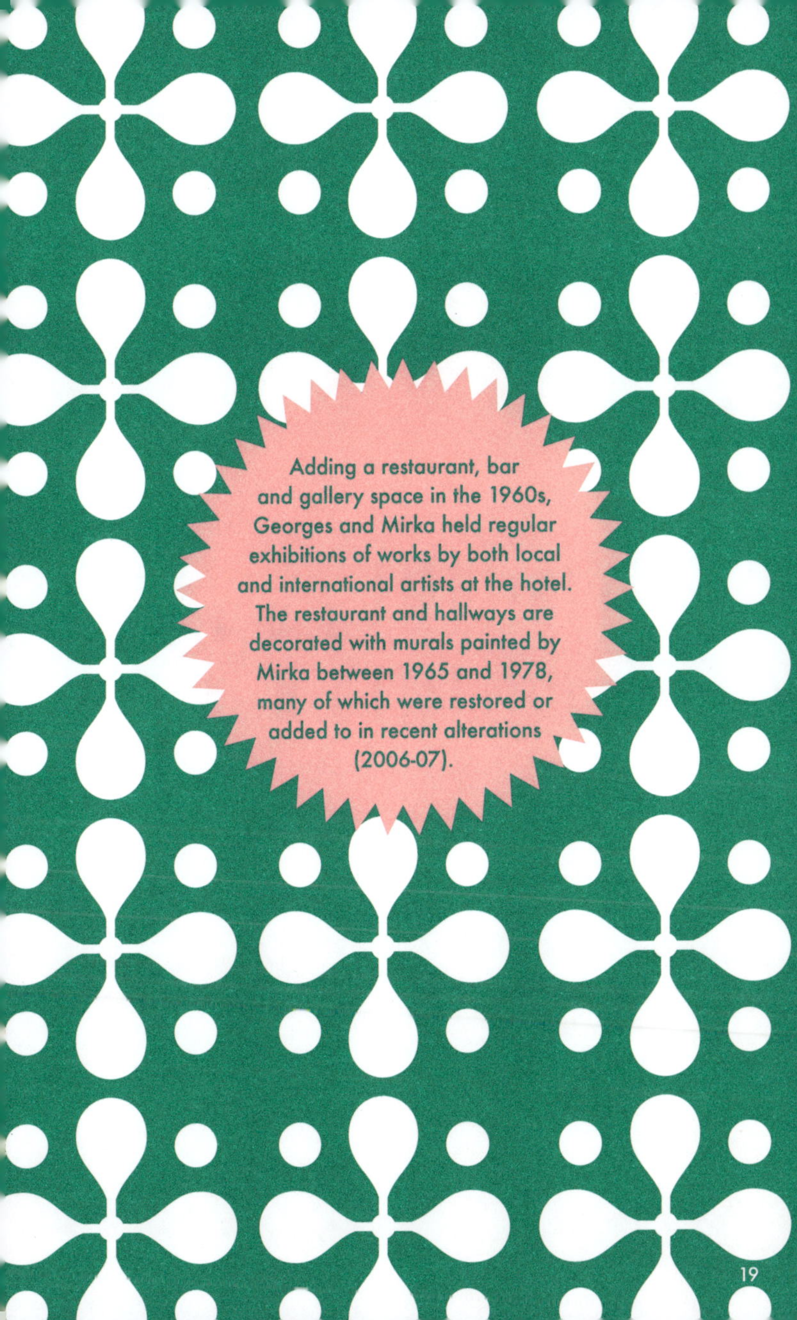

Adding a restaurant, bar and gallery space in the 1960s, Georges and Mirka held regular exhibitions of works by both local and international artists at the hotel. The restaurant and hallways are decorated with murals painted by Mirka between 1965 and 1978, many of which were restored or added to in recent alterations (2006-07).

3 3-7 the Esplanade / 1855

MARLI PLACE

Originally built as a residence for Justice Stewart Johnstone, this Victorian terrace was divided into flats in 1911.

Maintaining the original structure, this provided a central maisonette flanked by two attached buildings, each with a couple of self-contained units, one upstairs and one downstairs. An external staircase structure was also added to enable access to each individual flat.

4 11 the Esplanade / 1878

THE ESPLANADE HOTEL

Known as the 'Espy' to locals, the Esplanade Hotel has been a cherished landmark in St Kilda for over a century. Originally an exclusive residential hotel for the wealthy, it was altered in 1921 to include a lounge bar and ballroom for the entertainment of the middle classes. It soon became an important dance and jazz venue and has been one of the premier live music venues in Melbourne ever since.

Designed in the Italianate style, the original facade comprises a three storey block flanked by bays. The second floor has Romanesque arched windows and Corinthian order pilasters. The projecting front entrance portico is part of the 1921 alteration.

THE BENNIES
APART FROM
THE OUTSIDERS
HARRISON STORM
NECRO (USA)
RUSSELL MORRIS
NUDIST FUNK
ORCHESTRA
THANK YOU
THE ESPLANADE
HOME OF LIVE MU
RESID ENCIES
TUESDAY
BRIGHTSIDE
THURSDAY
COLLAGE
SUNDAY
BOTTLESHOP

In 1988 there was widespread concern that development proposals threatened the Espy. Community activism ensued and it is now classified by the National Trust.

5 13 the Esplanade / 1965

BAYVIEW HEIGHTS

With nine storeys containing 32 flats, Bayview Heights is typical of the mid-rise apartment buildings that were constructed in St Kilda throughout the 1960s and 70s. Designed by architect Sol Sapir, the brown brick building is given visual interest with the contrasting white balconies and inverted wishbone shaped entrance arch.

Interestingly, the apartment has a twin at the top of Alfred Square (3 Alfred Square), built at the same time.

6 1-2 Alfred Square / 1858/1855

VICTORIAN TERRACES

These two terrace houses are amongst the earliest surviving residential homes in St Kilda. During the 19th century the grassy square they face would have been surrounded by similar dwellings, most likely built in the same, relatively plain style. Number 2, 'Tranmere', is the oldest of the two, constructed in 1855, with the corrugated iron veranda added at a later date, possibly replacing a canvas structure.

Across the street is Alfred Square itself, named after Queen Victoria's second son, Prince Alfred, following his visit to Australia in 1868. In the middle of the square sits an elaborate memorial to those St Kilda residents who fought in the Second Boer War in South Africa (1899-1902). Unveiled in 1905, it is constructed of brick covered in faience (tin oxide glazed tiles) with Art Nouveau decorative motifs and lists the names of the soldiers who served and died in the conflict.

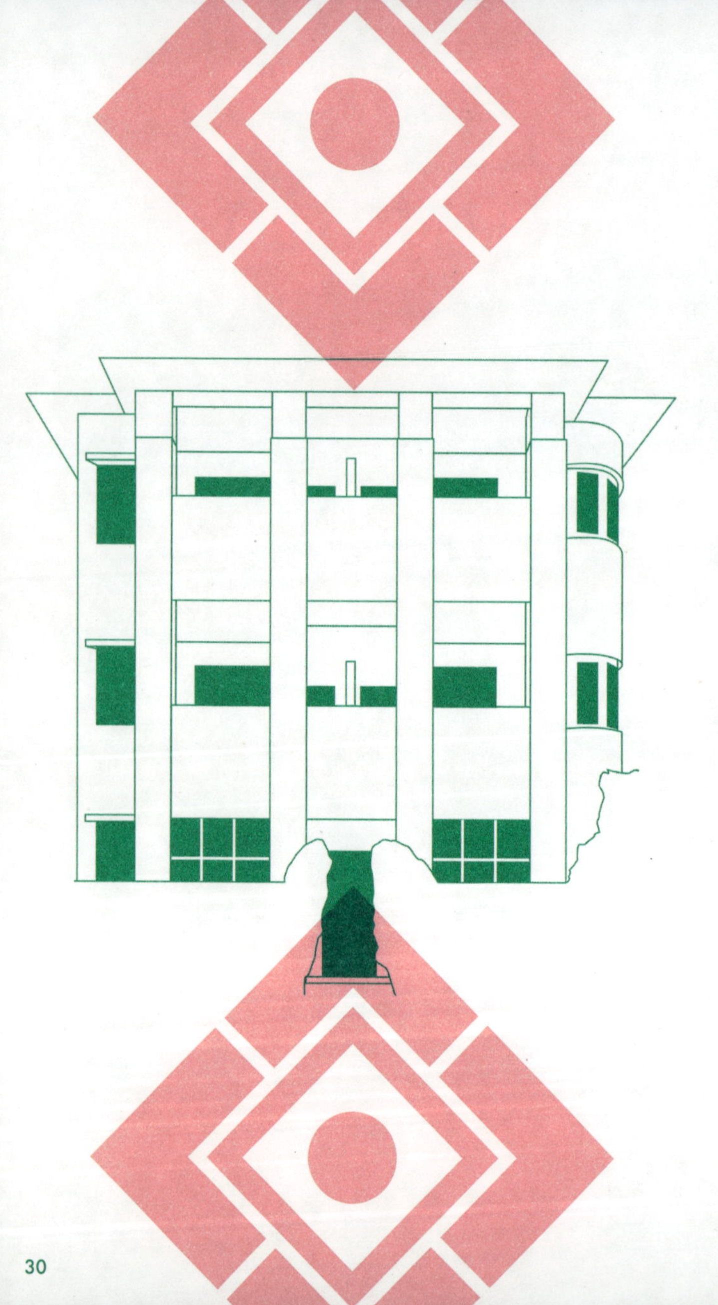

7 11 Wimmera Place / 1917

THE WIMMERA

Purpose built blocks of residential flats began appearing in St Kilda around the time of the First World War. Designed by architect Howard R. Lawson, Wimmera is a good example of the popular Arts & Crafts movement of the time.

With its un-rendered brickwork, shingle tile cladding and restrained decoration the building conforms to the notions of craftsmanship and honest use of materials that the movement sought to espouse.

The design has almost a proto-modernist quality as well, with the strong expression of simple geometric forms (cubic columns, cylindrical bow window structure, chimney) and general unadorned surfaces.

THE

8 14 Acland St / 1857

CHRIST CHURCH

Christ Church was completed in 1857 in a Neo-Gothic style and is the oldest surviving church in St Kilda.

Designed by architects Albert Purchas and Charles Swyer, it is constructed of Barrabool sandstone from Geelong with the interior featuring some of the finest ecclesiastical stained glass works in Victoria.

The surrounding Moreton Bay Fig trees were planted shortly after the church's construction.

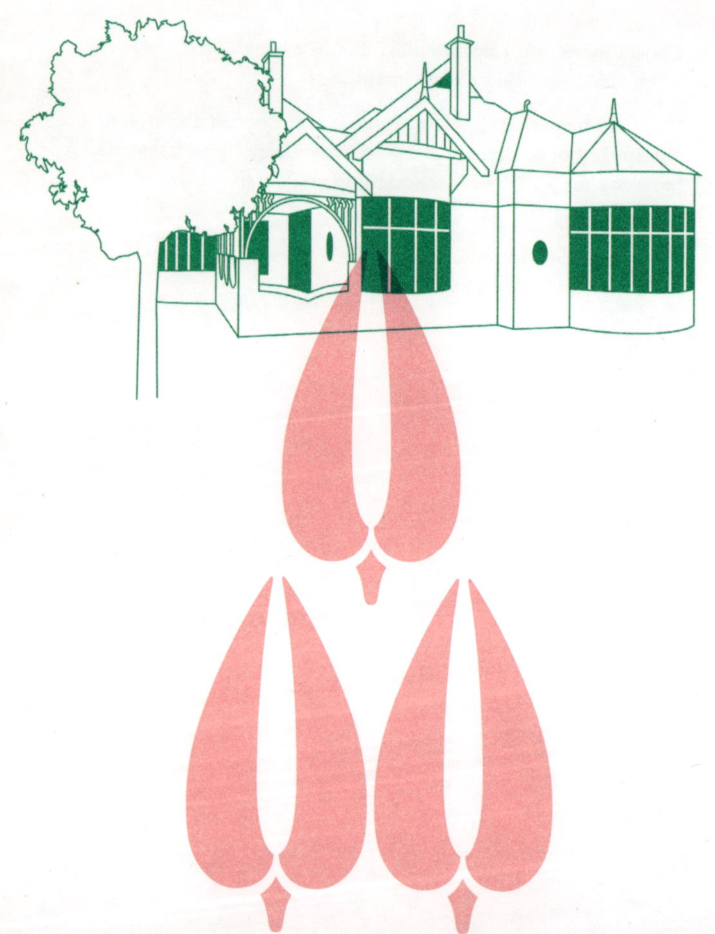

9 8A St Leonards Ave / c.1907

QUEEN ANNE HOUSE

St Leonard's Avenue was laid out on the site of a large estate which was subdivided in 1907. The mansion which sat on the estate was called St Leonards and was built in 1870 for John Matheson, general manager of the Bank of Victoria. Many of the houses subsequently built on the site were designed in the Queen Anne or Federation style, of which number 8A is a fine example.

Queen Anne was a revival style popular in the U.K, America and Australia from the late 19th to early 20th centuries. As the name implies it was a representation of architecture that existed around the time of the reign of the monarch (1702-1714) and, in Australia, often included features such as elaborate timber fretwork, circular windows, turrets and terracotta chimneys. It is a romantic, picturesque architectural style and this is certainly evident in the design of number 8A, with its complex terracotta roof detailing and tulip shaped woodwork on the fence posts.

Opened in 1887 by the Melbourne Tramway & Omnibus Company, the original route 96 was operated as a cable tram line along Bourke and Nicholson streets until 1940. Briefly replaced by a double decker bus service, the now electric trams were reinstated in 1955 and the line was extended to St Kilda in 1987.

Winding its way from East Brunswick to St Kilda (terminating at Acland Street) via the city and South Melbourne, route 96 has become extremely popular with locals and tourists alike. Carrying almost 40,000 passengers a day it is also one of the busiest lines in the network and is considered amongst the top ten tram rides worldwide.

6

10 4 St Leonards Ave / 1937

DEL MARIE

The Art Deco style first appeared in France after the First World War and rapidly gained popularity worldwide. Easily recognised by its repetitive geometric shapes, bold colours and rich ornamentation, the style evolved into various sub-genres throughout the 1920s and 30s.

Most notably, especially in relation to architecture, was Streamline Moderne which saw conventional Art Deco stripped of its ornament and an emphasis put on horizontal lines evoking speed and motion.

This, in turn, led to Nautical Moderne which further developed the motion theme using ship-related motifs as inspiration.

Designed by architect Stuart Hall, Del Marie (Spanish for 'on the sea') is an example of Nautical Moderne, a sub-genre of the Streamline Moderne style that was so popular throughout the world during the 1930s.

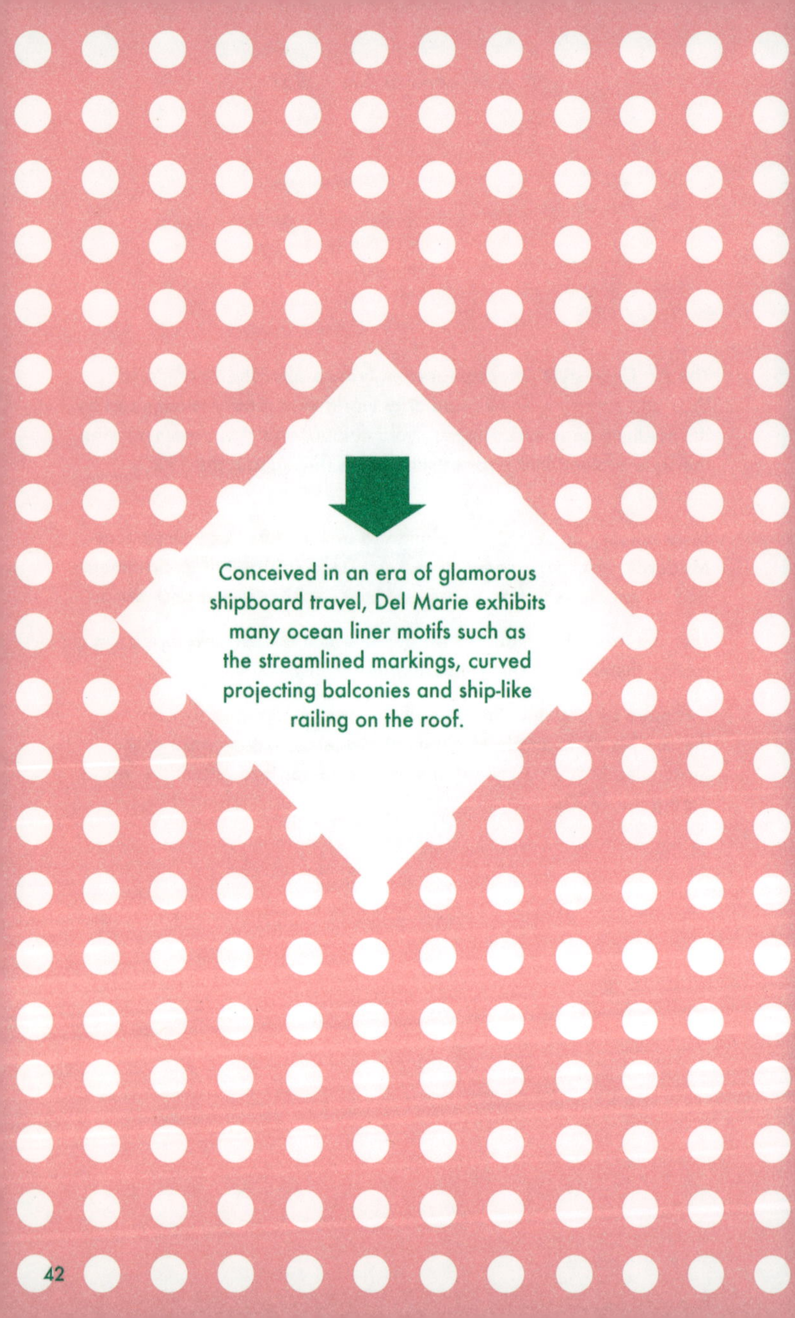

Conceived in an era of glamorous shipboard travel, Del Marie exhibits many ocean liner motifs such as the streamlined markings, curved projecting balconies and ship-like railing on the roof.

11 43 Acland St / 1926

ASTON COURT

During the inter-war period, residential architecture in Australia was influenced by exotic styles from both the New and Old Worlds. One was Spanish Mission from California and another was Mediterranean from Southern Europe. Although closely related, Mediterranean was seen as a more faithful representation of the architecture of Spain and Italy.

Aston Court, designed by Edwin J. and C.L. Ruck, is considered an example of this style with its arched loggias, white stucco exterior and pediment treatment.

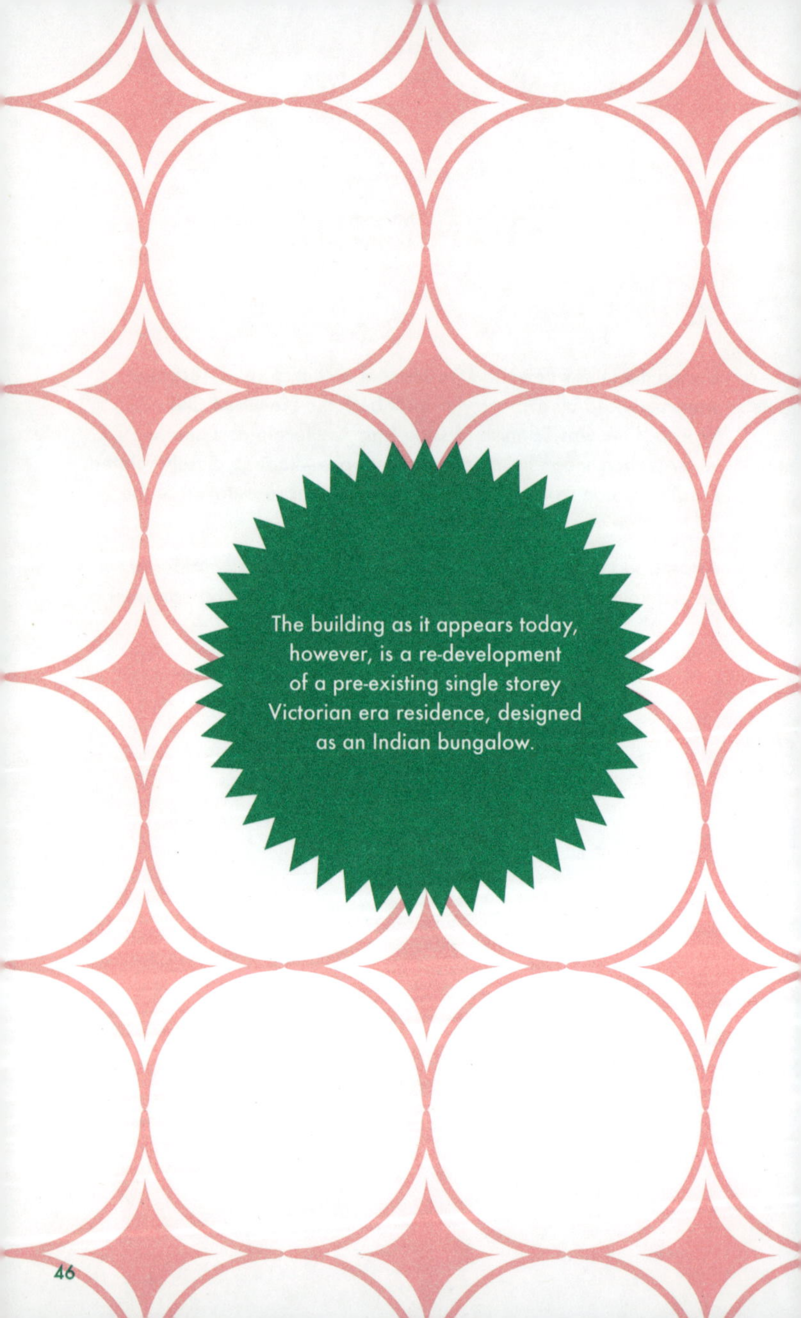
The building as it appears today, however, is a re-development of a pre-existing single storey Victorian era residence, designed as an Indian bungalow.

ASTON
COURT

12 45 Acland St / 1939

ACLAND HILL FLATS

Designed by architect Arthur Plaisted, Acland Hill represents an early appearance of the stripped back 'International Style' Modernism that was rapidly supplanting the more decorative architecture of the 1920s and 30s.

The cream brick block perched on Le Corbusier like 'pilotis' presents a bold, stark face to the street, while balconies and expressed stairwells project from the side in an almost industrial manner.

13 24 Acland St / c.1950s

BLOCK OF FLATS

With its tan brick construction, white framed windows and roof eaves, this block of 1950s flats appears like an enlarged post-war Australian suburban house of the period. Even the attached single car garage has been multiplied and clad with coloured slate, a typical decorative feature of period domestic architecture.

Access to the flats is through a central glass door, above which rises the staircase exposed by a glass curtain wall. The flats on either side have generous balconies with geometrically detailed railings.

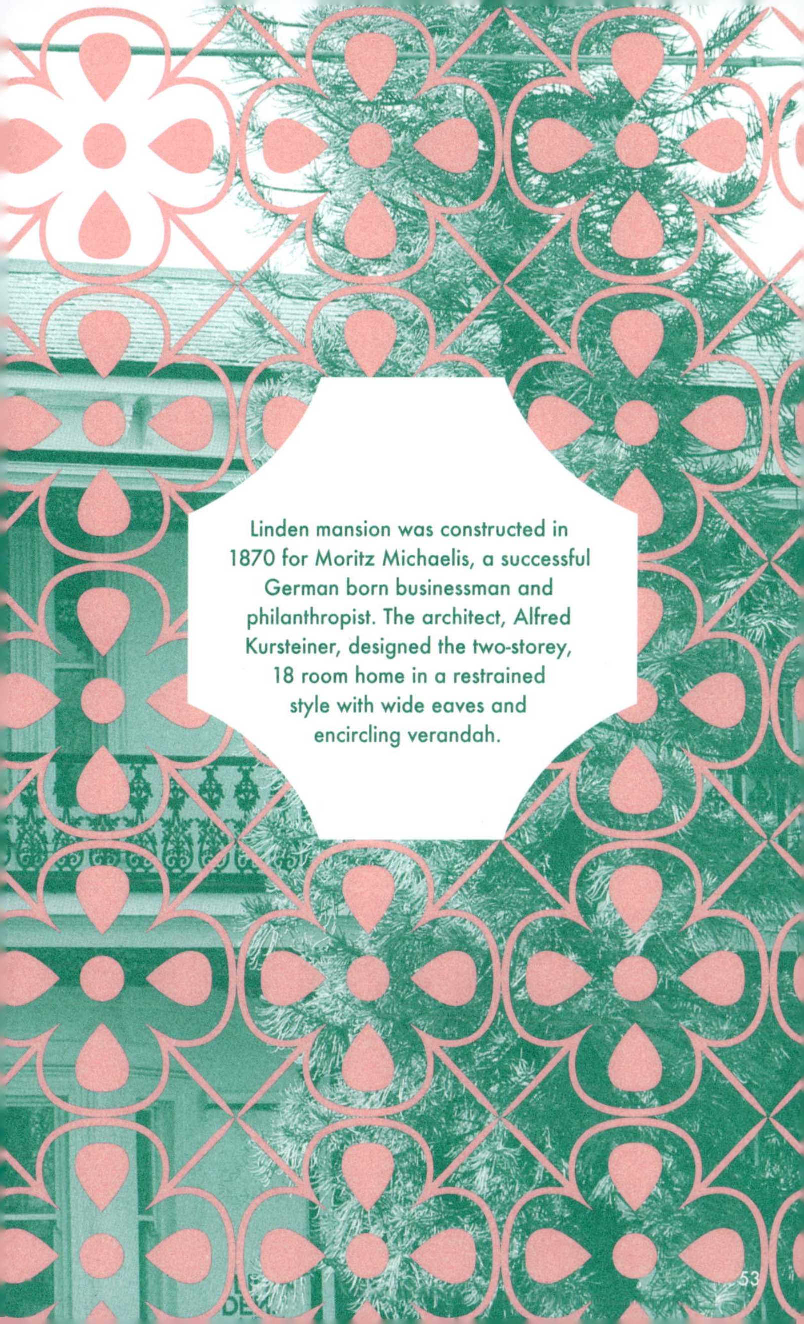

Linden mansion was constructed in 1870 for Moritz Michaelis, a successful German born businessman and philanthropist. The architect, Alfred Kursteiner, designed the two-storey, 18 room home in a restrained style with wide eaves and encircling verandah.

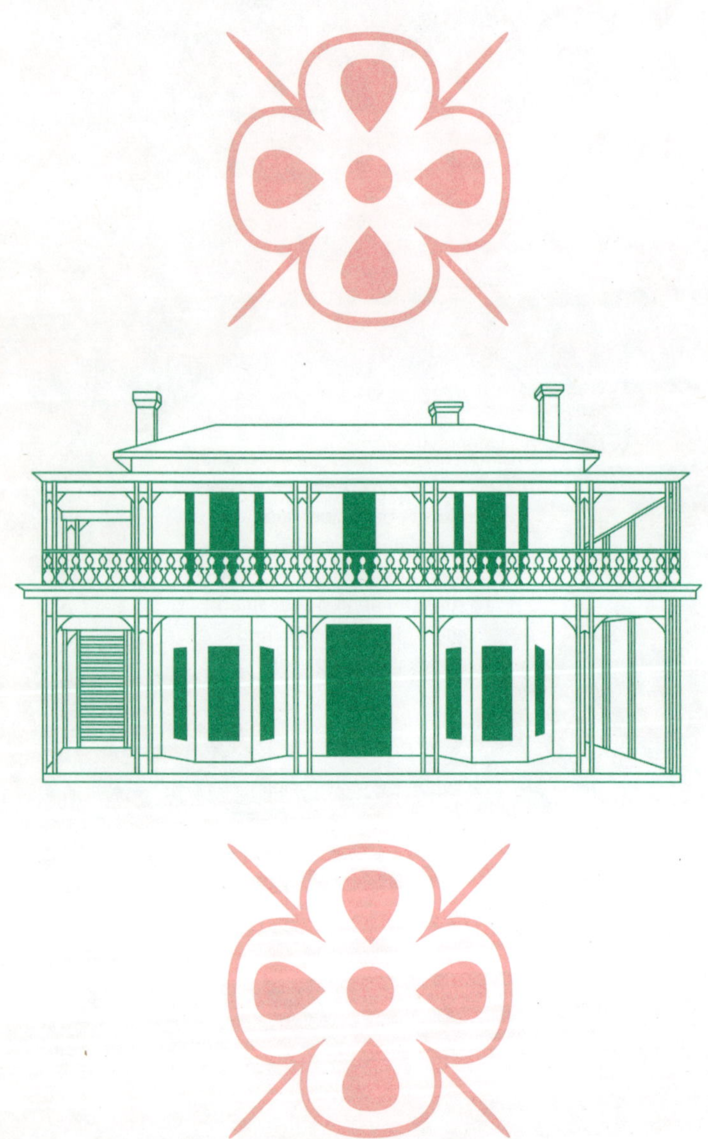

14 26 Acland St / 1870

LINDEN

With its slim double columns and delicate cast-iron lacework, Linden presents as a wonderfully elegant example of a mid-Victorian era mansion.

Unlike many St Kilda mansions after the 1890s economic bust, Linden remained in the Michaelis family until 1957. It then operated as a private hotel, known as Linden Court, until 1983 when it was purchased by the St Kilda City Council.

In 1986 it opened to the public as the Linden Arts Centre and Gallery and is open to visitors six days a week (free admission).

15 53 Acland St / 1886

HALCYON

Designed by architect Frederick De Garris, Halcyon comprises a two storey stuccoed brick structure dominated by the campanile inspired tower. The L-shaped verandah and balcony are decorated with slim cast iron columns and lacework, while the tower displays Corinthian order pilasters and ornate entablatures.

Shortly after Halcyon was constructed the economic boom became a bust and the grand mansion suffered the same fate as many others in subsequent years, operating as a boarding house for much of the 20th century. It is now, however, once again a private residence and remains a symbol, not only of a lavish architectural style, but also of the immense wealth that enabled such an indulgence.

Built well into the economic boom of the 1880s, Halcyon mansion is a good representation of the opulent late Victorian Italianate style (also known as the 'Boom style').

16 1 Robe St / 1932

THE ROYAL APARTMENTS

The Royal Apartments building is an interesting inter-war construction featuring elements from both Art Deco and later Moderne styles. The central arch design rises vertically in three layers in a Streamline manner, continuing above the roof to form a classically inspired pediment.

The glass panelling enclosing the internal staircase features geometric leadlight designs, while the horizontal aspect of the flats themselves is emphasised by delineated banding running along the flanking facades.

 18-20 the Esplanade / 1935

MANDALAY FLATS

The Mandalay Flats were constructed on the former estate of the 19th century mansion Rathlin. Comprising two wings with a central courtyard, Mandalay is a colourful example of residential Art-Deco architecture done in contrasting materials and textures of painted concrete and red brick.

The central entrance/staircase structures feature interesting vertical and horizontal decorative elements and geometric glass panelling in both the doors and windows.

MELBOURNE'S MOST
UNIQUE FUNCTIONS!
Events
NEW
EVENT
SPACES!

Inspired by the original Luna Park on Coney Island, New York (1903), American showman J.D. Williams opened the Melbourne version to a crowd of 22,300 people on 13 December, 1912.

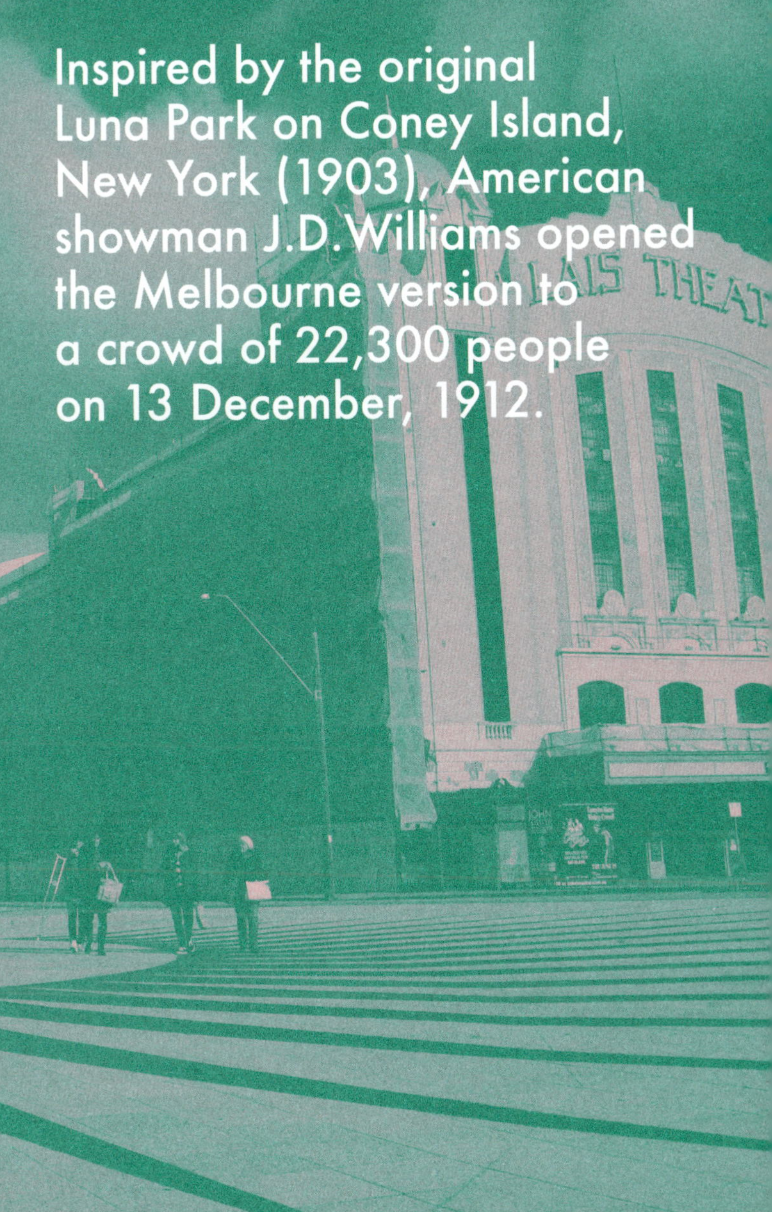

18 18 Lower Esplanade / 1912

LUNA PARK

The iconic 'Mr Moon' face entrance soon became a familiar and much loved sight to Melburnians and it has greeted generations of children and adults ever since. The entrance, with its flanking Moorish style towers (1912, restored 1999) and the Scenic Railway roller coaster (1912, the oldest continuously operating roller coaster in the world) are the only two remaining original features of the park. Other amusements and facilities have been replaced due to age or unpopularity over the years.

Four other Luna Parks were subsequently constructed around Australia from 1930 to 1944, however, apart from the one in Sydney (1935-present), all had closed down by the 1970s, leaving Melbourne's as the longest running in the country.

19 Lower Esplanade / 1927

THE PALAIS THEATRE

The Palais Theatre was originally designed as a cinema but, from the 1950s, increasingly became a live concert venue, a role it now almost exclusively performs.

Opened on 11 November, 1927, the Palais was originally commissioned and owned by the three Phillips brothers (Leon, Herman and Harold) from Washington. Leon Phillips had already established a successful portfolio of entertainment venues prior to the First World War, including a chain of Australia wide cinemas and Luna Park (in association with showman J.D.Williams).

The architect Henry E.White designed a grand establishment with a large Art Deco facade, flanked by projecting Moorish inspired domed towers (shared with Luna Park opposite). The towers exhibit classical detailing including small Doric order pilasters and scroll pediments.

With a capacity of 2,896 people the Palais is the largest seated theatre in Australia.

PALAIS THEATRE

20 12 Marine Parade / 1961

EDGEWATER TOWERS

Constructed in 1961, Edgewater Towers was the first privately developed high rise apartment block in Melbourne. Designed by architect Mordechai Benshemesh, the building rises to 44m (147 feet) and originally contained 100 flats, shops and a restaurant ('The Reef') on the ground floor.

By the 1960s Benshemesh was well known for his modernist apartment projects and the 13 storey Edgewater Towers was his largest design to date. Exhibiting the stripped back form of the International Style, with its plain surfaces and ribbon windows, the building nonetheless possesses a geometric texture with the occasional protruding bays and open balconies.

Although the individual flats and corridors have been extensively remodelled over the years the lobby still retains many original features such as the terrazzo flooring, blue and pink mosaic columns and a wall of Castlemaine slate.

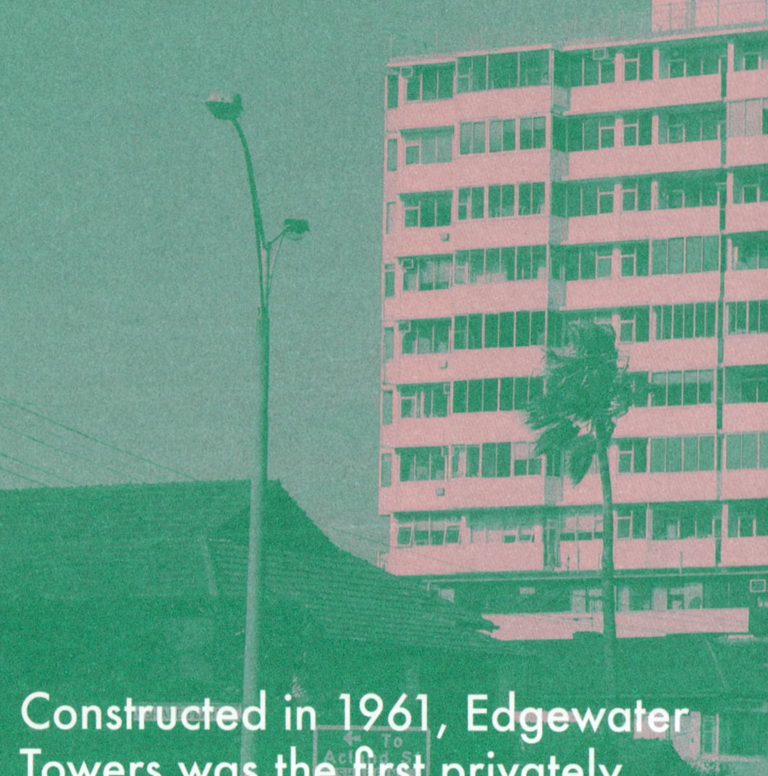

Constructed in 1961, Edgewater Towers was the first privately developed high rise apartment block in Melbourne.

EDGEWATER TOWERS

Acland CONTINENTAL CAKES
THE ACLAND CAKE SHOP
ALL CAKES MADE ON THE PREMISES
SAVOURY DELIGHTS • COFFEE • TEA • BREAKFAST

✪ OF NOTE

ACLAND STREET CAKE SHOPS

Heading towards the Village Belle hotel, on the right hand side of Acland St, are a selection of cake shops offering an impressive range of delicious cakes, pastries and other baked goods. Established by Eastern European Jewish immigrants in the 1930s, these purveyors of sweet treats have become an institution of Acland St and are well worth a visit for a coffee break.

21 202 Barkly St / 1891

VILLAGE BELLE HOTEL

The original Village Belle Hotel, a relatively simple single storey structure with a verandah, was built on this site in the 1850s. The present building was constructed in 1891 to a design by noted architect William Pitt, who was responsible for many grand buildings throughout Melbourne including the Princess Theatre (1886) and St Kilda Town Hall (1890).

Unlike many of his many Gothic and Second Empire inspired buildings, the Village Belle is reasonably restrained in design with its plain Romanesque style two storey structure wrapping around the corner of Barkly and Smith streets. The Barkly Street facade features an Italianate triple arched gallery (loggia) on the second level, above which sits a squared pediment.

The blue and white Orlando Wines sign dates from the 1950s.

ST KILDA PIER

The first wooden jetty was constructed off St Kilda beach in 1853 to assist settlers with the unloading of timber. This was washed away in a storm shortly afterwards and throughout the 19th century a more substantial pier was constructed and upgraded as both demand and trade grew.

The pier increased to its present size during the 20th century with the most recent concrete sections being added in the 1970s.

The kiosk located at the end of the pier was originally built in 1904 to a design by James Charles Morell. Officially named the Austral Refreshment Rooms, it was usually known by the names of subsequent vendors such as 'Parer's Pavilion' (as run by Francis Parer until the 1930s) and 'Kerby's Kiosk' (run by the Kerby family, 1934-1987).

On 11 September, 2003 the kiosk was almost totally destroyed by an arson attack but was rebuilt to the original plans using as much salvaged material as possible, including the cast iron roof, decorative cresting and the weather vane. It reopened in March, 2006.

With its French mansard style roof and classical symmetry, the quirky design can be viewed as a miniature representation of popular architectural styles of the time such as Second Empire and Moorish.

ST KILDA TIMELINE

1839 Grazier Benjamin Baxter becomes the first European settler in the St Kilda area (then known as Green Knoll).

1841 Area is officially named St Kilda with the first sale of Crown lands taking place a year later.

1848 The first St Kilda Cup horse race is held at a racecourse near the Village Belle Hotel.

1857 A railway line linking Melbourne to St Kilda opens.

1870-1890 St Kilda's population doubles to almost 19,000.

1901 The Duke and Duchess of York, on a visit to open the first national parliament, arrive at St Kilda pier, the entry point for many VIP guests to Melbourne.

1926 A February 10 fire destroys the Palais Pictures theatre, rebuilt as the Palais Theatre in 1927.

1941 American troops, many of whom would be stationed in the St Kilda area during the early years of World War Two, march down Beaconsfield Parade.

1956 Leo's Spaghetti Bar, one of Melbourne's first Italian restaurants, opens on Fitzroy Street in time for the Olympic Games.

1980 The inaugural St Kilda festival is held, beginning as an arts festival but eventually becoming a major Melbourne music event.

1987 The St Kilda railway line closes and is redeveloped as a light rail link, part of route 96.

THE WALK

The Footpath Guide to St Kilda Melbourne architecture takes approximately 45 minutes to 1 hour to complete.